Cantos, Incandescent

poems by

Rod Carlos Rodriguez

Finishing Line Press
Georgetown, Kentucky

Cantos, Incandescent

Copyright © 2024 by Rod Carlos Rodriguez
ISBN 979-8-88838-529-6 First Edition
All rights reserved under International and Pan-American Copyright Conventions. No part of this book may be reproduced in any manner whatsoever without written permission from the publisher, except in the case of brief quotations embodied in critical articles and reviews.

Publisher: Leah Huete de Maines
Editor: Christen Kincaid
Front Cover Art: Rod Carlos Rodriguez-"The Writer Prays for Inspiration"
Back Cover Art: Rod Carlos Rodriguez-"Writer's Inspiration Fulfilled"
Author Photo: Sabina de Vries
Cover Design: Rod Carlos Rodriguez

Order online: www.finishinglinepress.com
also available on amazon.com

Author inquiries and mail orders:
Finishing Line Press
PO Box 1626
Georgetown, Kentucky 40324
USA

Contents

COYOTE LULLABY 1
LUPE'S FINGERS 2
ISLA DEL ENCANTO 3
SHURFINE HOPES AND TAR PITS 4
BORDERS AND MUSES 5
MARTEL DESERTS 6
LAND'S END 7
JESUS OF THREE GAZES 8
LAND'S END AT HAOPILI TRAIL 10
OPEN DOORS AND TEARS 11
ASPHALT AND STONE, YEARS AND SOOT 12
SOIL AND ASHES 13
SPILL 14
CONCRETE YOGA 16
SUNLIGHT IN AMERICA 18
GULF WAR BLUES 20
DESERTS OF OIL AND BLOOD 21
NO MORE TICKETS 28
GOD OF FROGS 29
HERE AND NOW 30
GAIA IN RELIEF 32
WORDS, WORDS, AND CANTOS 33
COUNTING CORONA 34
IS A PAPER HEART 36
LETTING LUCY 37
FORGET HER BARREN GROVES 38

This book is dedicated to my wife, Sabina: it's just the two of us in this mad, mad world as we continue to rage, rage against the dying of the light.

Coyote Lullaby

Dawn paints his cheeks
in fluid pinks and greys.
Handcuffed to the rusted car's bumper,
night before last,

he listens
to coyote lullabies that
echo amid a Texas desert's
sandy-sweet fragrance.

Water bottle, still half empty,
rocks as a newborn
next to the sage bush and the ocotillo
ten feet away from a tongue swollen,

a mouth frozen in hundred degree
screams. And the dinero
he borrowed in Juarez for this passage,
it flies past the lullabies,

sails between cerveza symphonies
and topless lap dances
two nights before last.

Even as his breath is
a child's rasp, he caresses
pitted, sunburned lips.
If he's found,

maybe the blanqueador
of his bones will match
the pale stones
at his feet...

he wishes for one last lullaby.

Lupe's Fingers

Sees pudgy fingers, curl and release the air, she
pleads with la migra to bring back *Mama*, Lupe

shrieks against body armored Federales, forces
her to her knees, cuffs chafe Mama's wrists, tries to hold

her child's brown eyes, eyes covered with white hands,
delicate body convulses, shakes in rough grasps, captured

video promises viral coverage, media careers guaranteed
as agent plows his fist, Mama's teeth shatter, blood spills

on sun-dried border mud, her struggles weaker, head
rests against barricades, still focused on where her mijita

had stood, petite blue jeans, chanclas
fallen off when Lupe was fighting against

them, one rests upside down with a torn strap, Mama's broken
grimace, dry agony deep in her chest, still

her fingers, curl and release, convulse and ache for
Lupe's tiny begging, beseeching fingers.

Isla del Encanto

When dirty Ricardo in Spanish Harlem chews
his fingers raw and the food stamps
have run out for his mother,
will he still be raised
to love his white billionaire betters?

If Antonio stays in the projects and
takes that second or third job,
will his father keep dying from
the whiskey's cancer,
next to an alley in old San Juan?

If Oller's "El Velorio" dreams of
states in mourning,
will pouring over corpses and silencing
Rico's eyes grind down
old Spanish betrayal or Luiz Muñoz's
blind acquiescence for
paz en isla del encanto?

ShurFine Hopes and Tar Pits

He
waits,
his ShurFine
low rider parked
by the gas pump.

He knows the drugs
filled with sunsets
and waves crashing
against a reddish-pink sky
will arrive soon,
they always do.

He only has to wait
a little longer.
He'll refuse
the pills
covered in yesterday's
headlines,
stories of exceptionalism
and Howdy-Doody
time.

He'll settle
for aluminum balls
stuffed with tomorrow's
hopes sprinkled
over tar pits
and sour despots
lining their pockets
with fool's gold.

Borders and Muses

Feet planted, toes curl in dirt
between and around, a wide white line
plows the earth, divides one foot
from the other.

Grass undulates, hot breezes caress
among the blades, a sensual dance
by the edge of a glade, drawn whispers
breathe along one side of the border.

Rotted scrub brush, a patchwork next to
outcroppings, ocotillo blossoms blackened
next to crumbling cactus pads, and screaming gusts
blast through the other side of the border.

Arms extended in crucifixion, one hand grasps a gun
pointed at Liberty's temple, Her eyes
squeezed shut, waits for the weapons
bark to splinter bone and grey matter.

The other hand proffers
a branch from the olive grove planted
with Esperanza's brown hands, its leaves fat
with last spring's rain and tomorrow's sunshine.

Transfixed between the border,
Clio passes from the right ear to the left
and back, the words flood
these images, a kaleidoscope enlightened

and drowned at the same time.

Martel Deserts

A broken Martel station
by the tracks
grips the desert sand,
dark tattoos on its face
smile at the camera,
blackbirds flood a white cross
as a woman throws bread
next to empty wine bottles too many

miles from Paris,
too many lies
from the suited businessman
on a New York street corner
while above them,
in the high rise,
another woman sits
in an apartment she can't afford,
but the fruit drips on the carpet
as she exposes herself
to the tree of life.

The floods warp the houses,
the sky in Dali-esque colors
as they carry her lifeless
through the desert of roses,
hills in the distance
made of sleeping faces
as she rests
her legs across the
lion grass,
the air made of birds.

Land's End

There is a fold
in liminal spaces,
it shades still moments
slow to build
beneath our notice,
between our choices.
May we see
the stillness with
all our senses.
May it free us
in kind.

Jesus of Three Gazes

Martel Deserts II

Jesus of Three gazes
at their backs and
freezes as Sabina's
puppy of cotton

stares, surprised
by the Man of Spiders
taking his lunch break
outside the prison.

A paper-thin sports athlete,
Jose glowers at
old men walking
toward gourmet hot dogs,

but Maria keeps throwing
bread at the birds
in her cell,
frantic to get

out of the way.

She cries at the injustice
of Martel diners
lost to age and deserts,
and clouds hiding

dancing children
in flower print dresses.

Who decides when
borders are no longer
cages for a Maria, a Jose,
a Sabina…a Jesus of three gazes?

Land's End at Haopili Trail

Lava drapes
over molten fingers
grasping water's edge,
winds slice trees

sideways, desperate
for purchase among
heiau and rituals,
fixed in thunder
of waves and whale song,

Malekini dreams
and frozen tundras
scream their silence
if only we would

listen.

Open Doors and Tears

Now humid grass is moist today. The border wall is damp, too, with childish tears. Stephen Miller gives his daily affirmations in prayerful, blood-soaked hands. Who has forgotten this? None would remember this. Is this the new theme park ride? How many Brown kids will fit in the tent? When the cameras turn away, the talking heads talk of little more than moist dreams in stocks and 401k's. Here repeats the drills and calls to pray to united cages of these merry lies. They fly from mothers', fathers', tias', tios', abuelas' arms, so many arms cut down, dismembered. Fend off Winter's silver blankets clumped against the cement floor. Warehouses, old K-Marts, containers of human shit in full bloom. Soon Spring announces another year of arms disremembered, jutting through windows, crevices, doors. But the grass is still moist. The blades divide their green between asphalt curbs and coyote streets. Sheets of black and green are steaming amid yesterday's deluge and tomorrow's manhole, womanhole, person whole and holy. Pepper spray this talk with salty dancing close, very close that sweats through clothes and bedsheets and racy confessions. A murmur, a fervor drafted to close open doors, in walls, in moist days. Niña is afraid to touch the blade, the grass, all those fields promised, abuela, tio, Mamá, Papá, they promised. Miller's prayers go answered, a vengeance against janitors and abuelos, gone are the speed limits, limits at all. And news heads, fake eyes blind, mouths stuffed with cotton and whiskey screams that spray the rain, the moist torrential gully-washers.

Now dry grass engulfs the fire with tomorrow's childish memories. All those Millers and Mamás break under buses. Bones bleach under sol's stare. Bare dreams stay moist even if the river is ablaze. The tears are ablaze, raze these K-Marts, play in these barren fields. Open these doors. Open her tender, moist eyes.

Asphalt and Stone, Years and Soot

For My Children and Grandchildren

And who loses? If the silence becomes so loud it chains the bed to the floor
in knots, the curtains will weep past breaking. Dead messages flash across
screens and frames, *you don't love me, a real father would take care of me,*
his voice cracking, betrayed and enabled at the same time by empty
that's your mother talking! You give her too much power…
words, only words that echo, settle along highways hiding distance,
paper boundaries cemented in asphalt and stone. Writing years that separate,
sluice the vicious *he's your grandson and you'll never see him, ever,*
a fjord dammed against roots, planned in dense droughts swimming
between pinpricks bleeding me dry.

Who loses? When the air's vacuum chokes the laughter vibrating in polaroids
fading, always fading small, brown hands losing their grasp past needing
a father, past eyes blurred by silence, the violence of its calm. A psalm to
loss plagued with birthday after birthday pouring down *10 years, 20 years,
30 years young no more.* Torn arms, legs, lying flat in Gobi sands rolling
over the wind's furnace that burns, rushes those gaps in memory holding
bus rides to Nana's house, finding lost cries at Sea World, binding
blood with the soot left in the fireplace, blown away and leaving me,
alone.

Soil and Ashes

Gets in the bones, icy tendrils deep in the marrow even before the machine has stopped. Even before prayers and nonsensical "lived a good life" or "loved by so many" or "hated like no other." Then the soil, it makes a soul-deep thump, gathers and accumulates by degrees, granules assuming a deep frost en masse, black muffles "in o-r hea-ts a-d minds" or "Go- w-ll prov-de" or "a l-sson to -s all," of gathering dirt punctuating the growing, chill stillness. Voices, distant, faint, understood more for their receding presence, than for any clear notions. Muscles begin to break down, mold takes root, blossoms in the mouth, the eyes, the heart. The arms that held: sons and a daughter, a belt to beat them, grudges against the children's absence, these arms melt into cold fabric of the casket. Legs, which carried the body to one bar after another, one drink to the next, bow and darken, eaten from without by worms and bacteria. The brain: last to ashes, last to love, last to bring surcease to childish scrapes or fights over why "you never deserved us!" or a mother's reproachful "Why didn't you see him at the hospice?" It remains in these glacial, soundless frames of our regret.

Spill

There are poems in high gloss, silk satin,
and mat finish—dribbled on the floor
while painting the room
in off-white and grey,

these poems are small splats and
bigger dollops in baby blues, rumbling reds,
quiet chocolate, and cinnamon abbreviations,

turpentine cannot wash them away,
scrubbing only spreads their
message, inuendo, and liminal
reach to all corners, and now

I've tracked their wisteria purple
and dandelion yellow to other
areas of the house, on

stoops outside, in cobblestones
of once immaculate streets,
foxfire-red-verses invade police stations,
cerulean-sky-blue-rhymes pepper

town halls and once grey-neutral
federal buildings. My haiku handprints
celebrate on flag poles in sunset orange and hunter

green. These poems stain sidewalks with
lazy pinks, fuzzy-maroon-pantoums drizzle
on Covid-empty arenas and
cast a pall over silver sparkling highways,

rainbow-plaid-rivers rush through
valleys glowing in gold and copper sonnets,
pour into luminescent lakes rippling

over my iridescent living
and breathing room

Concrete Yoga

Old town frozen,
forlorn houses,
train tracks still
bear the trains' weight,

a studio,
hidden behind old homes,
a large and full-throated sign,
declarative and sure,
faces small town
attitudes and thinking.

Monster trucks and
water towers hover
nearby, reminds
those within this studio
how new age this

yoga thing is.
Unwavering,
they still
wave hello to
close-minded neighbors at
the gas station,
the grocery store.

Town center,
close in its disquiet,
suspicions linger in silence.

This concrete has set,
Its rebar of open minds
and breath strengthens

and fortifies
souls, in harmony,
in peace

with yoga of concrete.

Sunlight in America

Morning light has soared
my sky and sanctified,
healing from pyres
of fear, love so bright
my freedom shakes,
it rises from chains
broken,
to bandage and mend
my bleeding wrists,
my voice sings
even as the night
slowly fades
from bullets
that silence no more.
Always,
ALWAYS!
We will keep fighting
against manifest destiny,
against white privilege
and the raping of culture,
of language.
Lives we're losing
to Covid, police brutality,
racial hatred will
drive us forward.
Now rising up,
for lost voices
like a George Floyd,
a John Lewis, a
Breonna Taylor.
Mother Earth's smile
glimmers in hopeful
oceans turned
aquamarine, viridian,

we gasp the air, finally
free of jesters
no longer laughing.
We MUST
always light
our paths,
varied and diverse
to dispel baleful
shadows,
embrace unity,
and toss
all those clowns
into pits of their
own filth!
…rise.
…Rise!
RISE!
Our voices are FREE!
May it EVER, ever be!

Gulf War Blues

Back is the semaphore thudding strikes between C5 and C6 along the spine, a fractal filigree
Tam-tam-ambulating chords of blood and bone and calcified cushions progressing to years
spent prone on heating pads, leading back to the Rodriguez curse, a hex plastered across
sore shoulders and neck muscles forced into menial shoveling, harvesting, carrying, groveling
stacks of bodies piled in front of Amazon, the Waltons, a Bezos.

Cracked is the rigamor-tis, seizing winged scapula, Nerves damaged amid nerve agent inoculations, a government-issued petri dish broken in four, five, nine places and spreading, falling, falling, down veteran-forgotten pits, craters mark invisible knives making daily visits along with muscle spasms, thrumming, humming, emptying Tylenol bottles, Ibuprofen, Bayer aspirin, packing echoes of pain for future encampments atop my aching back.

A lack in caring for legitimate, proven liability in Gulf War grievances laid out in pain doctors, physical therapists, spinal surgeons, flailing and pantomiming and dancing the VA games, hoops, denials, appeals, judges feverish and focused on anything but the 25 years of pain, depression, and screaming *NO MORE*! Let the calcified cushions, winged scapula, pantomiming appeals plow the cemetery's sigh-sigh-silent wait for this pain. No. More.

Deserts of Oil and Blood

Held my newborn
son close.
Whispered apologies,
more for me,
in my baby's ear.
War came to
my door. Zachary's infant
snores echoed
through the visit.

Last kiss for my
older son,
calling after me,
Anthony's three-year-old
plaintive *Daddy*
knifing my heart,
again and again.

This war for oil,
invasion, and lies,
these reasons
fail under stark
light of day,
the drums call
soldiers, airmen,
marines, sailors,
men, women,

poor, middle class
families, we fight for rich men
safe in houses
of white and gold,
for profit, with blood
spilled in deserts and bomb raids,
brothers and sisters,

cousins and nephews,
nieces and uncles,
daughters and aunts,
fathers,
mothers,
no longer

waiting at home,
now strapped
in canvas seats on
C130's, C17's,
M16 hands,
9-millimeter hips,
we all cry with
our personal
reaper, breathing,
rasping, kissing behind
our ears, bone hands
gently rest on shoulders.

We're warned,
expect random
cells of violence,
from Saudis and others.
Guard against
their hatred, especially
of Western women,
how dare they bare
hair and skin,
beneath chocolate-chip
uniform.

Depression sets in
as C-17 wheels
hit tarmac. White,
pock-marked buildings,
under 100 degree
daylight, convoys
announce American
target practice and
incoming! screams
over radio static.

A nightmare, from
the beginning, the shared
American compound
is scant protection, drilled
exercises, killed insurgents
catch tickets to Allah
and 72 virgins promised,
betrayed. We eek what
life we can, between
attacks, pretend, deny,
salute crisply at
our commanders.

Pain in shoulders,
my back. Arm doesn't
work. Who threw the grenade?
Don't remember hearing
an explosion. Just woke
with searing, piercing,
glass-shattered-beneath-the-skin
agony. American doctor
referral to Saudi clinic.
Waiting, watching,

men in one area,
women, Saudi or foreigner,
in another. Heat, stink,
close bodies, copper smell,
Saudi father gently rests
his hand on his young son.
Fear stands between us,
behind our stares.

I think of my
sons, of home, the smiles
when I tickle
their bellies,
doctor calls my name,
his accent garbles
Roedriiigezzz.
Poked with anxiety and
needles, waiting, pain,
watching, pain, pin cushion,
pain, guinea pig, *American swine
should be put down...*
spoken in the hallway.

In my quarters, sand everywhere,
always seems to
get in, just need
a beer, a strong drink,
to forget, just a moment,
no alcohol permitted,
against our host's *religion*,
but we fight
their wars, we kill their enemies!
Oil, always, the oil.

Downtown Riyadh,
need to break the
monotony, drills, and false
alarms, obey public
dress code when not in
chocolate-chip
camo.

The 5-times-a-day
prayer bell blankets
the city. Devout Saudi men
race for the nearest
mosque. Saudi women hide,
anywhere, avoid tourists.
One Saudi woman decides
to kneel and hide
no more.
An alcove of
a closed jewelry

store entrance,
her black
robe becomes soiled,
still kneels, places forehead
to sand and cement,
I witness this quiet
rebellion, I fear for
her life, unable to move,
unable to call out,
the men in the mosque

race out,
try to find the rebel sinner
in wind tossed abaya,

but she becomes the wind,
she is the desert sand,
whipped away.
I breathe, I relax,
I wait, I watch.

City square,
families, festive
air circles
a dais,
reddish-brown
bloodstains streak down
a block of stone,
a drug dealer,
brought out to
screaming, jeering
voices, the stumbling
hooded man is forced
to his knees,
blubbering, begging,
voice and words
are slurred, drugged.

A large,
crescent blade
is released, muscled
arms lift the
silver and scribed
cleaver, movements quick,
precise, I stand transfixed,
the crowd's ecstasy
drives the blade
through neck muscle and sinew.

Return to my quarters.
Sleep. And sleep.

Fellow airman,
wears government-issued
abaya, she is circled
by male airmen,
we act as
guards, Mutawa prey
on foreigners, these
religious police
beat the sinful,
use sticks wrapped
in tape,
We wait, we watch,
we walk, a shield
against this nightmare,

and return to America.

Sleep. And sleep.
Hold my boys.
Sleep.

Tried to leave
the desert where
it was.
It came with me.
Remains everywhere.
And the nightmares.

For oil,
always, for oil.

No More Tickets

At the state fair:
a dirty, torn stuffed bear…
a broken Ferris wheel leans
sideways, slowly decays.

Shattered, scattered fun-house mirrors
glitter as the stars near
rusted carny trailers.
Ring-toss bottles
remain piled haphazardly
against the pie-eating contest
stand and the pin wheel ride.

Dented, pitted by storms
and age, the carousel
lays quiet, still.

And old, state fair flyers
blow over everything…never rest.

Last ticket sold
years ago.

God of Frogs

A hotel page
placed him here,
his gaze takes
in guests, luggage,
crying children.

His color vibrates
depending on his
mood, currently
the blues are very bright.

Inches away,
a glass pane
separates him from

tree leaves,
rocks he could
rest beside.

But the potter
who made him
gave him no lungs
or nostrils,

no way to be
what he was made
to be, the Frog God
told by tribes peopled
by myth and legend.

Still, he vibrates,
now in colors
of red and aquamarine.

Here and Now

Here and There

And there, Breonna went to sleep. She was tired from a long shift at the hospital. She received the gratitude of a body riddled with police bullets in her bed. Rosey flowers of blood bloom beneath her. And here, Eric needed some extra money by selling cigarettes. He was met by a police chokehold, gasping his last breath. His last thought was the flowers he planted that might be blooming in the garden he loved so much, hoping their green leaves will help someone else to breathe. And there, Tamir loved playing with his toy gun, pretending he was justice in a small town protecting the little park area from any *bad guys*. A sheriff's bullet ended Tamir's playtime without any warning, his 12-year-old heart pumping his blood, creating red carnations in the snow where he lay dying. And here, George didn't have anything smaller than a $20-dollar bill for his cigarettes. The police officer's knee kept George from thinking about whether or not the $20 was counterfeit. A small filament of blood escaped his nose as his last breath was for his mother, begging to breathe.

Somewhere and Elsewhere

And somewhere, American protests are spreading as fast as a COVID bouquet. Both the police and federal agents' tear gas blossoms in streets burning for a George and a Breonna, a Tamir and an Eric, an Andy Lopez, a Sandra Bland, a Mike Ramos, a Carlos Ingram López, and so many more. And elsewhere, Murder hornets took their decimated and beheaded honeybee hives and went home. They saw how fucked America was and wanted none of it. And somewhere, Karens and Kevins are screaming at being told to wear masks. They're screaming at multi-hued people in parks, at pools, at grocery stores, at Starbucks just for *living* while hues of the rainbow. Karens and Kevins too concerned with these inconvenient truths taking their sacred freedoms to shoot and maim and dominate lesser people of colors resplendent and rich. And elsewhere, the desperate climate is still changing, flexing its muscle in menace and malice billowing through earth's mantle. Gaia's mood is frothing and boiling oceans, Her silent cries ignored as poison grows on delicate reefs.

Right Then and Right Now

Right then, you changed your mind by realizing your privilege and fragility were ingrained. They were kneaded and massaged into your alabaster skin the moment the doctor snipped that umbilical cord. They were watered and fed with downpours and sun-drenching ultraviolence.

Right now, another Rod Carlos Rodriguez or Maria Lopez or Anthony Baez is waking up to lives rendered broken, sabotaged, *denied* the promise that all men (women, LGBTQ+) are created…equal? Are there different levels of equal? Is equal planted solely amid finer homes and security in your city on a hill, devoid of color? Right then, booths are being made ready for the shit show. Lines will form rainbow petals that circle buildings, streets, and cities. They will shape and curl into the largest human constellation of events in history. Right now, plans are being fashioned around planets and stars that taunt our dreams. Needles of fire will sprout through sand and cement steeling resolutions eyeing Luna, arching for Ares.

Here and there. Somewhere and elsewhere. Right then and right now.

Gaia in Relief

Ripples in paper oceans reflect the copper sun's glare,
sold in aging paperback poetry books, words
burnished in rust red and seasonal gold
inside coffeeshops and libraries, Half-Price Book stores,
and a pub in Southampton, UK.

Ripples in this poem, copper in my sea,
celebrate a Muse and her curse of words in me.
Lochs of ice and distance, sealed in simple dreams,
earthen mounds and images shaped in figurines.

Stanzas flood Gaia and drown in emerald depths,
bought with puerile bubbling photographs, images
streamed in transparent negatives and treasonable groves
outside city limits, Bexar County seats, Enchanted Rocks,
and a Jim's diner off highway 1604.

Stanzas buy plug nickels in buffalo silver sheets,
lazy lyres and tragic deaths beside Salado Creek,
Whistles steam above me, groves with rocks beneath
highways rising above my deserts in relief.

Words, Words, and Cantos

*after "Words Words" by Iris M. Zavala,
translated by Roberto Marquez*

Cantos, cantos
sung to diseased politicians
with oil-black irises
shaped in bullion,
American flags
draped on
mustangs crashing
in Ponce, San Juan,
it's 2021,
long dead
sugar factories,
naval kill zones
in Vieques,
earthquakes and Jurakán
crush Humacao,
Fajardo, and Caguas.
The drums,
Covid silent,
puertoriqueños in misery
vomit their hate
of politicians or
flags,
streets flooded
with regurgitated
breakfasts and café con leche,
where la colonia
seethes and bleeds,
mas cantos, we beg.
We sing.
Sing.

Counting Corona

He's sitting up today. The machines make their usual beeps, breaths, groans. The cough is muted, a bit. I can see a little more light behind his eyes and a weak smile, just for me. Lucy, his usual nurse wearing blue scrubs, is counting to herself again, behind the mask. She doesn't think I can hear her whispered cadences on my computer screen. Even after just six days since José was admitted, I find solace in Lucy's counting. José motions the nurse to bring the camera on the laptop closer to him. The stale sweat, the mucus sliding down the back of his throat I imagine smells horrible to Lucy. I clutch the corners of my computer screen, feel its sharp edges dig into my flesh. Today I will not cry. He must see strength from me. *Helena, I feel a little better*, his voice grates against the plastic walls around his bed as he looks at me through the camera. Just this small effort tires him out. *You're such a trooper, José*, I respond. No, no tremble that I can hear in my voice. Lucy keeps counting.

The doctor calls at 2 am. *José is on pure oxygen now.* I wipe the sleep out of my eyes, guilt craters the lining in my stomach for drifting off. I look at the computer screen, hear his coughs, hardly a pause between breaths. *I'm here, José, I'm here!* He barely turns his head; this starts another coughing fit. Lucy is not in the room. The machines are counting for her with beeps, breaths, and groans. José settles down, finally. And my tears, finally. The computer screen grows cloudy as my cheeks are gouged with wet streaks, eyes staring, waiting. With the machines.

The moment José is placed on the ventilator is when I start feeling a tickle in the back of my throat. At least he's not coughing anymore. Lucy is back with her counting wearing peach-colored scrubs this time. The machines breathe, beep, and groan for him. I find myself breathing with their rhythm, through the computer's speakers. I manage a weak *I love you, José*. Lucy says he can't hear me. I don't believe her. I thought I saw his leg move. I count the Tylenol in my hand. The doctor emails me the *just-in-case* paperwork. He says I need to sign it and email it back as soon as possible. I wish Lucy would stop counting.

is a paper heart

forcing itself to pump 3x5 index card-beats per minute? Do the paper cuts on surrounding organs imply that your feelings are any more real than a meat-sack heart? Internal bleeding of hope rests in your belief something would carry the pleasure of knowing, just that knowing might make a difference. A difference of none, according to those measured card-beats per minute, per second, per the flaps of sparrows raining their noon-shouting and -fileting of yesterday's newspapers made of fish. Your knowing churns in that construction-paper stomach, pulping any reason to drown the acid reflux fear, painting intestines in soupy watercolors, vivid acrylics, and frozen tempera. Colors that run, colors that spread and know the fear, the knowing sopping through plaster-of-Paris-kidneys leaking and crumbling in flakes and rivers of white gypsum. Fear and knowing. Knowing and fear. That slick, yellowed magazine-quality paper puddles, pools, and spills on cardboard tiles, growing and bulging their stains that no amount of formula 409 will get out. And you know. You stopped being afraid. You just know.

Letting Lucy

Counting Corona II

Lucy listens to the clock on the wall. It runs on AA batteries. She's had to change them a few times. Her patients in the ICU love and hate how she counts the second hand. The loud clicks slam and explode in her head. *Slam! 1, Slam! 2...* She is ready to quit today. Corona has killed more people here than she remembers. *Slam! 3, Slam! 4...* Joe, an orderly from the ER, passed through the ward. He lasted 2 weeks. *You did your best.* It's what the doctor is *supposed* to say. She doesn't believe him. *SLAM! 10, SLAM! 11...* She counts aloud. It helps lessen the blow of each secondhand hammering in her skull. And this patient; she looks at the chart. A José Rivera who croaks at his wife, Elena, Helena, or something like that. Lucy grudgingly brings the computer closer to Mr. Rivera. She decides to come in tomorrow. Give it another day. *Slam! 50, Slam! 60.*

Joshua in the next room coughs and coughs...Lucy always waits for the second or third round of Josh's cacophony. He never disappoints. There's no clock in his room. She can close her eyes a little if it weren't for the damn machines, their beeps, and groans, and the coughing. Lucy quietly counts the coughs. *Hack! *one* Cack! *two** Is there a believable excuse to not come in tomorrow? Lucy adjusts the IV. Stares at Josh's once handsome nose and chin. His face contorts with each cough. Lucy needs a break. Next shift break is in an hour.

Mrs. Rivera is crying again. Lucy's lost count of the woman's weepy fits. No battery in the clock. Lucy is tired and is still ready to quit. One of the staff nurses left Mr. Rivera's legs hanging off the bed. Really does look like the leg keeps moving. Machines keep breathing, beeping, groaning. They're Lucy's new clock. *Breath 1, beep 2, groan 3...* Mrs. Rivera's coughs through the computer act as a counterbalance. Lucy's ready to inform the head nurse she quits. *Cough 8, cough 10...* She even has a plan. She'll wait for Mr. Rivera. He's almost done.

Forget Her Barren Groves

—in mirrored flowers growing behind frames,
ornate in 14 carats and lamb's wool.
—in reflected fire burning a sunset's photograph,
bleeding with 3rd degree Detroit rust.

—by white lilies crawling over Saturday's gardening sheers,
sharpened on pooling Saharan pebbles.
—by filigree fences crumbling Sunday's betrayal,
frail in 100 years of God-filled lies.

—deprived of dormant streams babbling in soundless veins,
blazing Her parched lavender fields, fallow.
—deprived of suitors dressed in honey or pollen one spring,
savored among dry and blackened Oregon forests.

ACKNOWLEDGMENTS

"No More Tickets"—*Arts Alive San Antonio* (2020)
"Lupe's Fingers"—*Good Cop/Bad Cop*—Flowersong Press (2021)
"Martel Deserts"—*Words4Birds*—Audubon Society (2021)
"Borders and Muses"—*Border Arts: Beyond the Barriers*—The Raving Press (2022)
"Open Doors and Tears"—*Border Arts: Beyond the Barriers*—The Raving Press (2022)
"Isla de Encanto"—*Voces Cósmicas: April is the Coolest Month*—Hijo Del Sol Publishing (2023)
"ShurFine Hopes and Tar Pits"—*Voces Cósmicas: April is the Coolest Month*—Hijo Del Sol Publishing (2023)

Rod Carlos Rodriguez has an M.F.A. in Creative Writing from the University of Texas at El Paso and is a Lecturer at the University of Texas at San Antonio Writing Program. He is an award-winning poet who has been writing for over 40 years. He has 3 published books of poetry: *Exploits of a Sun Poet* (Pecan Grove Press, 2003), *Lucid Affairs* (Sun Arts Press, 2012) and *Native Instincts* (Human Error Publishing, 2016). He is founder/chair of the Sun Poet's Society, South Texas's longest running weekly open-mic poetry reading (1995-2022). He was nominated for the San Antonio Poet Laureate in April 2012, April 2014, April 2016, and April 2018. He was the poetry editor for *Ocotillo Review*, a literary journal/periodical and he was the editor of the *Texas Poetry Calendar 2023* (Kallisto Gaia Press).

www.ingramcontent.com/pod-product-compliance
Lightning Source LLC
Chambersburg PA
CBHW020343170426
43200CB00006B/492